My Sticker Dictionary

A fun-filled dictionary with
activities to complete!

This dictionary belongs to

How to use this book

You use a dictionary to find the meaning of a word or to check how to spell it. This sticker book contains a range of activities to help you become familiar with a dictionary.

Large letters mark where each new letter of the alphabet begins. Color the uppercase letter and sticker the lowercase letter.

Use the **panel letters** to find the correct page.

Each entry starts with a **headword**. These words are in alphabetical order. When two words start with the same letter, the second letter decides which one comes first, and so on. Use the **headwords** to check how a word is spelled.

large (adjective)
larger, largest
If something is **large**, it
is **large**. The opposite

The **part of speech** tells you if a word is a noun, adjective, or verb. A noun names something, an adjective describes something, and a verb tells you what someone or something is doing.

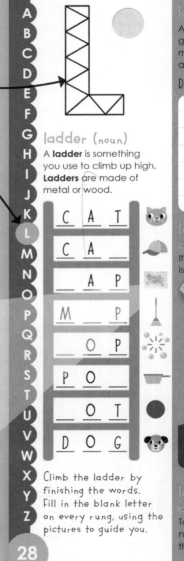

A B C D E F G H I J K L M N O P Q R S T U V W X Y Z

28

Climb the ladder by finishing the words. Fill in the blank letter on every rung, using the pictures to guide you.

C A T
C A
A P
M   P
O P
P O
O T
D O G

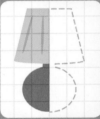

lamp (noun)
A **lamp** is a device that gives you light. You can move a **lamp** around and switch it on and off.

Draw the other half.

ladder (noun)
A **ladder** is something you use to climb up high. **Ladders** are made of metal or wood.

large (adjective)
larger, largest
If something is **large**, it is is **large**. The opposite of

laugh (verb)
laughs, laughing, laughe
To **laugh** is to make noises because you think something is funny.

The **definition** tells you what the word means.

2

We use special words to **compare** things. Find out how to spell them here.

light (adjective)
lighter, lightest

1. If something is **light**, it does not weigh much. It is easy to

Plurals name two or more of something. Unusual plural spellings are shown here.

Verbs change depending on whether we are talking about the past, the present, or the future. Find the forms to use here.

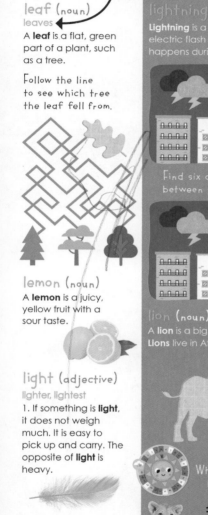

leaf (noun)
leaves

A **leaf** is a flat, green part of a plant, such as a tree.

Follow the line to see which tree the leaf fell from.

lemon (noun)
A **lemon** is a juicy, yellow fruit with a sour taste.

light (adjective)
lighter, lightest

1. If something is **light**, it does not weigh much. It is easy to pick up and carry. The opposite of **light** is heavy.

2. If something is **light**, it has pale colors. The opposite of **light** is dark.

lightning (noun)
Lightning is a bright, electric flash that happens during storms.

Find six differences between the scenes.

lion (noun)
A **lion** is a big, wild cat. **Lions** live in Africa and India.

What is a baby lion called?

3 21 2
___ ___ ___

listen (verb)
listens, listening, listened

To **listen** is to pay attention to a sound or to what someone is telling you.

lizard (noun)
A **lizard** is a type of animal with four legs and a long tail.

long (adjective)
longer, longest

If something is **long**, its ends are far apart. The opposite of **long** is short.

a b c d e f g h i j k l m n o p q r s t u v w x y z

29

Follow the instructions to complete the **activities** on each page.

When you see a gray shape, find the correct **sticker** on the sticker sheets.

When you see this icon, use the **code wheel** to complete the activity. (See p. 64 to learn how to make and use the code wheel.)

When you see this icon, **color** the picture, shape, or letter.

airplane (noun)

An **airplane** is a flying machine that carries people and things.

alien (noun)

An **alien** is a make-believe creature from space.

Draw the other half.

alligator (noun)

An **alligator** is a large reptile that lives in rivers and other wet places.

Find six differences between the scenes.

alphabet (noun)

An **alphabet** is a collection of letters that is arranged in a special order.

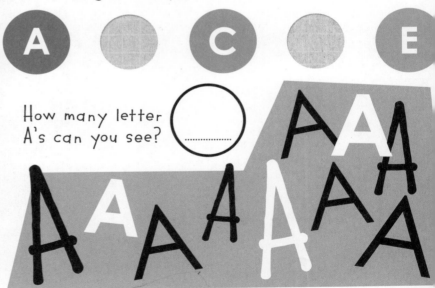

A   **C**   **E**

How many letter A's can you see? ....

ambulance (noun)

An **ambulance** is a vehicle that takes hurt or sick people to hospital.

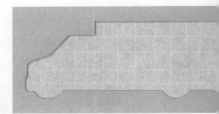

anchor (noun)

An **anchor** is a heavy metal object that is lowered from a boat when it stops, to keep it from drifting.

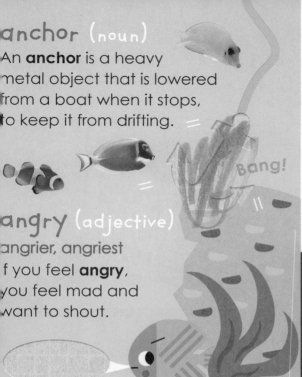

Bang!

angry (adjective)

angrier, angriest
If you feel **angry**, you feel mad and want to shout.

animal (noun)

An **animal** is a living thing that moves and eats. Zebras, snakes, sharks, birds, and bugs are animals. Plants are not animals.

Join the dots.

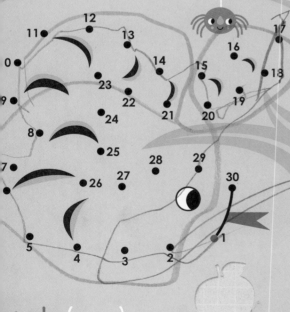

apple (noun)

An **apple** is a round, juicy fruit that grows on a tree. Its skin can be green, red, or yellow.

arrow (noun)

An **arrow** is a stick with a sharp point. You can shoot an arrow with a bow. You can also draw arrows to point out the way to go.

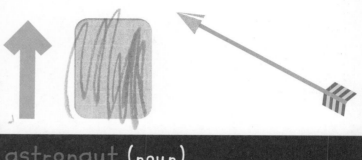

astronaut (noun)

An **astronaut** is a person who travels in space.

What planet did the astronauts go to?

13 1 18 19

baby (noun)
babies

A **baby** is a very young person.

ball (noun)

A **ball** is a round object used in games. You can throw, catch, bounce, roll, or kick a **ball**.

basket (noun)

A **basket** is a container used to store or carry things.

bat (noun)

1. A **bat** is a piece of wood that is used to hit a ball in a game.

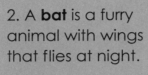

2. A **bat** is a furry animal with wings that flies at night.

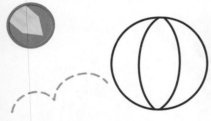

Guide the bat through the maze.

Start

What is the bat saying?

<u>2</u> <u>15</u> <u>15</u>

___ ___ ___

beach (noun)
beaches

A **beach** is a sandy or pebbly strip of land at the edge of the ocean.

beautiful (adjective)

more beautiful, most beautiful

If something is **beautiful**, it looks or sounds lovely.

The beach was beautiful.

bed (noun)

A **bed** is something you rest and sleep in.

bicycle (noun)

A **bicycle** is a vehicle you ride. It has two wheels and pedals.

big (adjective)

bigger, biggest

If something is **big**, it is large. An elephant is **big**. The opposite of **big** is small.

birthday (noun)

Your **birthday** is the day of the year on which you were born.

boat (noun)

A **boat** floats on water and carries people and things.

What rhymes with bat? Fill in the missing letters to finish the words.

B	A	T
C	D	T
M	A	B

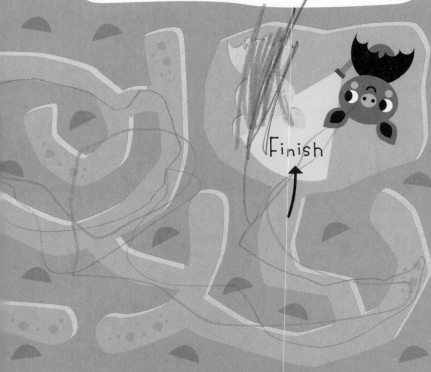

Finish

a b c d e f g h i j k l m n o p q r s t u v w x y z

book (noun)

A **book** is made up of many pages held together inside a cover.

Fairy Tales

box (noun)

A **box** is used to hold things. Most **boxes** have straight sides and are made of plastic or cardboard.

boy (noun)

A **boy** is a child who will grow up to be a man.

bread (noun)

Bread is a food made with flour. It is baked in an oven.

Circle the one that doesn't belong.

bridge (noun)

A **bridge** is a structure built over a river or road. We use it to cross to the other side.

Find six differences between the scenes.

brush (noun)
brushes

A **brush** has lots of stiff hairs or wires and usually has a handle.

Circle the one that doesn't belong.

bucket (noun)

A **bucket** is used to carry things, such as liquids or sand.

Circle two buckets that match.

build (verb)

To **build** is to make something by putting parts or materials together.

Draw a line to match the correct-shaped brick to the hole in the wall.

bulldozer (noun)

A **bulldozer** is a big machine with a curved blade that pushes rocks out of the way.

Unscramble the letters to see what it picked up.

B I R K C S

B I R K C S

bus (noun)

buses

A **bus** is a long vehicle with seats inside to carry people around.

Guide the bus through the town to the park.

← Start

→ Finish

butterfly (noun)

butterflies

A **butterfly** is an insect with large, colorful wings.

buy (verb)

buys, buying, bought

To **buy** something is to pay money for it so you can own it.

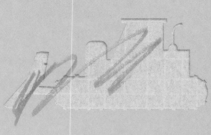

What is on the shopping list?

2	15	15	11	
2	15	15	11	

2	18	5	1	4
2	18	5	1	4

2	18	21	19	8

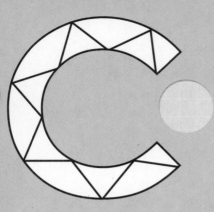

cake (noun)

A **cake** is a sweet food. It is often made by mixing butter, sugar, eggs, and flour, and then baking the mix in the oven.

calculator (noun)

A **calculator** is an electronic machine used for figuring out math problems.

calendar (noun)

A **calendar** is a chart showing all the days, weeks, and months in a year.

call (verb)
calls, calling, called

1. To **call** someone is to speak loudly so they notice you.

2. To **call** someone means to phone them.

Hello!

Ring ring!

camel (noun)

A **camel** is a four-legged animal with one or two humps on its back.

camper (noun)

A **camper** is a large vehicle in which you can sleep and cook meals when camping.

cap (noun)

A **cap** is a soft, flat hat without a brim, sometimes with a visor in the front.

car (noun)

A **car** is a vehicle with four wheels and an engine. We use cars to get from one place to another.

card (noun)

A **card** is a folded, decorated piece of stiff paper sent on special occasions.

cartoon (noun)

1. A **cartoon** is a short film using animation rather than real people or objects.

2. A **cartoon** is a funny or exaggerated drawing.

Press out the stencils and draw your own cartoons!

WOW!
ZAP!
HELLO

Sticker funny things on the faces.

What is the superhero saying?

<u>26</u> <u>1</u> <u>16</u>

_ _ _ _ _

cat (noun)

A **cat** is a four-legged animal with soft fur, sharp claws, and a long tail. People keep small **cats** as pets.

Copy the cat. Use the grid to guide you.

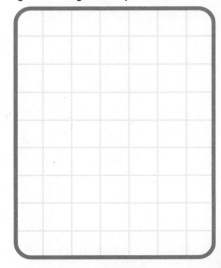

catch (verb)
catches, catching, caught

To **catch** something is to grab hold of it while it is moving.

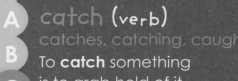

caterpillar (noun)

A **caterpillar** is a long, thin insect. It grows into a butterfly or a moth.

cereal (noun)

1. A **cereal** is the grain, or seeds, from a plant such as wheat, corn, or rice.

2. **Cereal** is a breakfast food made from wheat, rice, or oats. You often eat it with milk.

chair (noun)
A **chair** is a seat with four legs and a back.

cheese (noun)
Cheese is a food made from milk.

child (noun)
children

A **child** is a boy or girl who has not yet grown up.

chocolate (noun)
Chocolate is a sweet food made from cocoa beans.

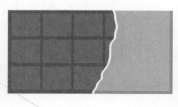

city (noun)
cities

A **city** is a big, busy place where many people live.

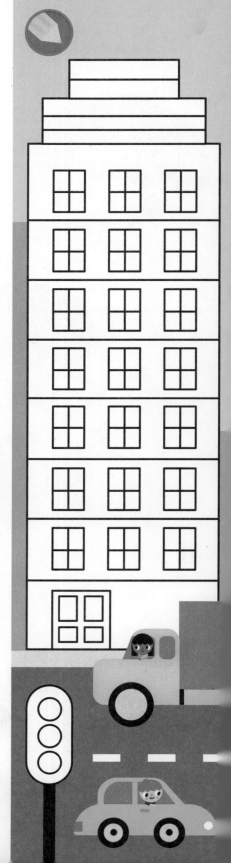

clean (verb)

cleans, cleaning, cleaned

To **clean** something is to wash it so that it is no longer dirty. The opposite of **clean** is dirty.

Join the dots.

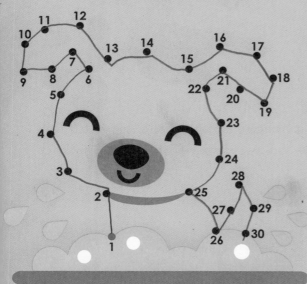

clock (noun)

A **clock** is a machine that shows you what time it is.

Draw the small hand on the clocks to show the time given.

1 o'clock   6 o'clock

Trace the time on the clocks below.

What noise does an alarm clock make?

18	9	14	7	18	9	14	7

clothes (noun)

Clothes are the things that people wear, such as shirts, pants, and socks.

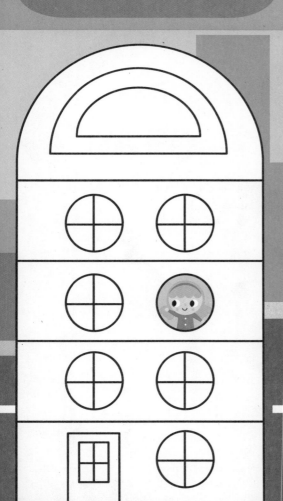

a b c d e f g h i j k l m n o p q r s t u v w x y z

coat (noun)

A **coat** is something you wear over other clothes. It keeps you warm when you are outside.

cold (adjective)

colder, coldest

If something is not warm or hot, it is **cold**. Ice cream is **cold**. The opposite of **cold** is hot.

Draw the other half.

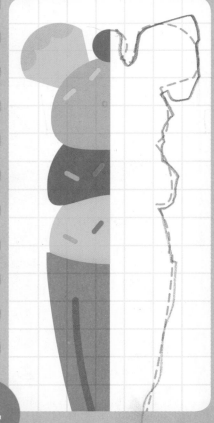

color (noun)

Red, blue, and yellow are **colors**. By mixing them together, you get other **colors**.

Blue + yellow make green.

Color the blue and yellow paint flows. Find the missing stickers at the end of the flow to see what other colors they make when mixed.

What does ⬤ + ⬤ + ⬤ make?

2 18 15 23 14

___ ___ ___ ___ ___

comb (noun)

A **comb** is a piece of plastic or metal that has lots of thin teeth. You use a **comb** to untangle your hair.

computer (noun)

A **computer** is a machine that stores information and helps people work and keep in contact.

cow (noun)

A **cow** is a large female farm animal that produces milk. The male animal is called a bull, and the baby is a calf.

crawl (verb)

crawls, crawling, crawled

To **crawl** is to move around on your hands and knees. Babies **crawl** before they can walk.

crocodile (noun)

A **crocodile** is a scaly animal that looks like an alligator. It has sharp teeth, short legs, and a long tail.

How many crocodile shapes can you see?

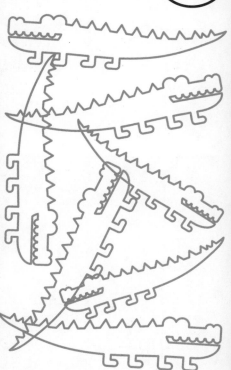

crown (noun)

A **crown** is a kind of hat, usually worn by kings and queens. It is often made of gold or silver.

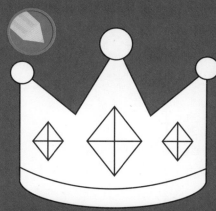

cry (verb)

cries, crying, cried

To **cry** is to be so sad or hurt that tears fall from your eyes.

cut (verb)

cuts, cutting, cut

To **cut** something is to open or break into it using scissors or a knife.

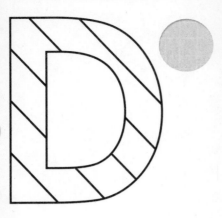

dentist (noun)

A **dentist** takes care of people's teeth.

desert (noun)

A **desert** is a dry place without many plants.

dessert (noun)

A **dessert** is a sweet food you eat at the end of a meal.

Follow the line to see which dessert the boy chose.

dinosaur (noun)

A **dinosaur** is a kind of animal that lived millions of years ago.

dirty (adjective)

dirtier, dirtiest

If something is **dirty**, it has mud or stains on it. The opposite of **dirty** is clean.

The dinosaur is dirty.

doctor (noun)

A **doctor** is someone who takes care of people who are sick or hurt, helping them to get better.

dog (noun)

A **dog** is a four-legged animal that is often kept as a pet. Most **dogs** bark.

How many dog toys can you see?

....

donkey (noun)

A **donkey** is a furry animal that looks like a small horse with big ears.

draw (verb)
draws, drawing, drew, drawn

To **draw** is to use pencils, pens, or crayons to make a picture.

Can you draw...

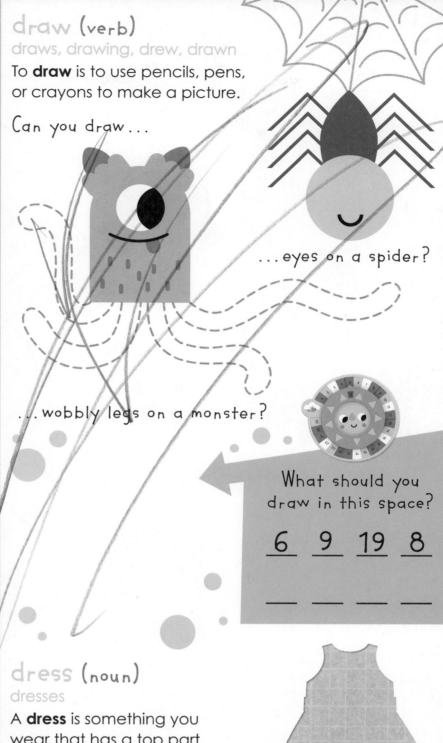

...eyes on a spider?

...wobbly legs on a monster?

What should you draw in this space?

6   9   19   8

___ ___ ___ ___

dress (noun)
dresses

A **dress** is something you wear that has a top part joined to a skirt.

drink (verb)
drinks, drinking, drank, drunk

To **drink** is to swallow a liquid, such as water, milk, or juice.

Circle two drinks that match.

eagle (noun)

An **eagle** is a large bird with big wings, a curved beak, and sharp claws.

earth (noun)

1. The planet we live on is called **Earth**. It is also called the world.

2. **Earth** is another word for soil.

eat (verb)
eats, eating, ate, eaten

To **eat** is to chew and swallow food.

Follow the lines to see who ate each snack.

What is on the menu?

MENU

16 9 26 26 1

___ ___ ___ ___ ___

19 15 21 16

___ ___ ___ ___

egg (noun)

Many animals, such as birds, lizards, and some fish, live inside **eggs** until they are big enough to hatch out.

Sticker the animals in the eggs, then write the animal names underneath.

S _ _ _ _

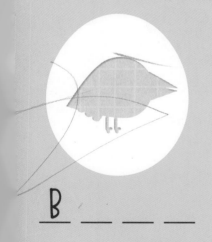

B _ _ _ _

F _ _ _

elephant (noun)

An **elephant** is a large animal with tusks, big ears, and a long nose, called a trunk.

Which shadow belongs to this elephant?

empty (adjective)

emptier, emptiest

If something is **empty**, it has nothing inside it. The opposite of **empty** is full.

Draw some cookies to fill up the jar.

envelope (noun)

An **envelope** is a paper cover, or container, you put letters or cards inside.

evening (noun)

The **evening** is the time between the afternoon and nighttime. In the **evening**, it starts to get dark.

Find six differences between the scenes.

A B C D E **F** G H I J K L M N O P Q R S T U V W X Y Z

family (noun)
families

Your **family** is the group of people closest to you. Your parents, sisters, and brothers are all part of your **family** even if you don't live together.

farm (noun)

A **farm** is a place where people grow food and raise animals.

feather (noun)

Birds have **feathers** on their bodies to keep them warm and dry. **Feathers** are light and help birds fly.

fire (noun)

A **fire** is the hot, bright flames made when something is burning.

fire truck (noun)

Fire trucks are vehicles firefighters use to drive to fires.

fish (noun)
fish, fishes

A **fish** is a type of animal that lives in water. **Fish** have fins to swim and gills to "breathe" underwater.

flower (noun)

A **flower** is the part of a plant with petals. Many **flowers** smell nice and have bright colors.

Draw the other half of the flowers.

20

fly (verb)

flies, flying, flew, flown

To **fly** is to move through the air without touching the ground. Birds, planes, and helicopters **fly**.

Find the words in the word search. Words can go across or down.

1 balloon

2 bird

3 kite

4 plane

	d	p		s		
e	b	l	w	b	e	z
c	d	m	k	a	m	n
p	l	a	n	e	l	p	k	l
u	p	s	y	t	l	u	i	a
e	f	t	p	o	z	t
b	i	r	d	o	r	e
	c	a	y	n	f
	p	l	a

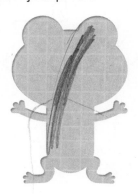

frog (noun)

A **frog** is a small animal that lives in damp places. It has large back legs and can jump far.

fruit (noun)

A **fruit** is a part of a plant that holds seeds. Many **fruits**, such as apples and grapes, are juicy and good to eat.

full (adjective)

fuller, fullest

If something is **full**, it has so much in it that there is no more room. The opposite of **full** is empty.

food (noun)

Food is what you eat. It keeps you strong and healthy.

fork (noun)

A **fork** is a tool used for eating. It has sharp, pointed ends and a handle.

Circle two forks that match.

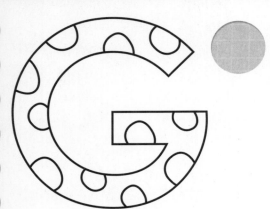

game (noun)

A **game** is something you play for fun. Chutes and Ladders is a **game**.

Play the games on this page with a friend.

Play three games of tic-tac-toe.

Who won the most games?

What game is the girl playing?

<u>3</u>　<u>8</u>　<u>5</u>　<u>19</u>　<u>19</u>

___ ___ ___ ___ ___

To play Dots and Boxes, each player takes turns to draw one line between two dots. When a player connects four lines, they make a box. The winner is the one who draws the most boxes.

Press out the pairs game and play it with a friend.

TOP TIP!

When you complete a box, draw your face inside it.

garden (noun)

A **garden** is a place where people grow grass and other plants.

gate (noun)

A **gate** is a type of door in a wall, fence, or hedge.

giraffe (noun)

A **giraffe** is a tall animal with a spotted coat and a very long neck.

Draw six spots on the giraffe.

girl (noun)

A **girl** is a child who will grow up to be a woman.

glasses (noun)

People wear **glasses** over their eyes to see better or to protect their eyes from the sun.

Circle two glasses that match.

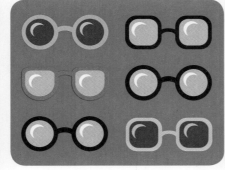

goat (noun)

A **goat** is an animal with long hair and horns on its head. It looks a little like a sheep.

grape (noun)

A **grape** is a small purple or green fruit that grows in bunches. **Grapes** are used to make wine.

grow (verb)

grows, growing, grew, grown

When somebody or something **grows**, it gets bigger.

gymnastics (noun)

Gymnastics is a sport and exercise in which you use strength and balance to do different movements.

Which shadow belongs to this gymnast?

H

half (noun)
halves

When something is broken into two pieces the same size, one piece is called a **half**.

Draw the other halves.

hamster (noun)

A **hamster** is a small, furry animal with a short tail. Some people keep **hamsters** as pets.

Guide the hamster through the maze to his cage.

Start →

↓ Finish

A hamster stores food in its ...

$\underline{3}$ $\underline{8}$ $\underline{5}$ $\underline{5}$ $\underline{11}$ $\underline{19}$

____ ____ ____ ____ ____ ____

happy (adjective)
happier, happiest

To feel **happy** is to feel joyful or pleased. The opposite of **happy** is sad.

hat (noun)

A **hat** is something you wear on your head.

Search the grid for the word "hat."

a	k	h	a	t
h	a	t	r	h
a	m	a	h	o
t	r	h	a	t
c	d	a	h	e
h	a	t	h	a
a	c	o	a	r
h	a	t	t	u

How many can you see?

heavy (adjective)

heavier, heaviest

If something is **heavy**, it weighs a great deal and is hard to carry. The opposite of **heavy** is light.

helicopter (noun)

A **helicopter** is a flying machine with blades that spin around. It can move straight up from the ground and hover in one place.

hen (noun)

A **hen** is an adult female bird.

hide (verb)

hides, hiding, hid, hidden

To **hide** something is to put it where other people cannot find it. You can **hide** a thing or you can hide yourself.

Find five eggs hidden in the hen house.

horse (noun)

A **horse** is a large, strong animal with four legs that people ride or use to pull things, such as carts.

hot (adjective)

hotter, hottest

If something is not cold or warm, it is **hot. Hot** things can burn you. The opposite of **hot** is cold.

house (noun)

A **house** is a building where people eat, sleep, and live. **Houses** have roofs, walls, doors, and windows to keep the people inside warm and dry.

ice (noun)

Ice is frozen water. It is cold, hard, and slippery.

ice cream (noun)

Ice cream is a sweet, creamy frozen food made from milk.

igloo (noun)

An **igloo** is a small, round house made from blocks of ice.

Draw a line to match the correct shape to the hole in the igloo.

insect (noun)

An **insect** is a small animal with three body parts and six legs. Many **insects** have wings. Ants, beetles, butterflies, and bees are all **insects**.

Follow the lines to see who landed on the flower.

jacket (noun)

A **jacket** is a short coat that people wear to keep warm.

Draw the other half.

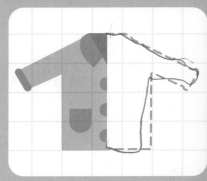

jaguar (noun)

A **jaguar** is a big, wild cat with black spots. It lives in the Americas.

jeans (noun)

Jeans are pants made from tough material called denim. They are often blue.

jellyfish (noun)
jellyfish

A **jellyfish** is a sea creature with a soft, round body and long tentacles.

Which shadow belongs to this jellyfish?

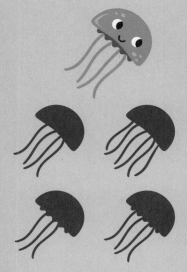

jigsaw (noun)

A **jigsaw** puzzle is a game made from lots of flat pieces that fit together to make a picture.

juice (noun)

Juice is the liquid that comes out of a fruit when you squeeze it.

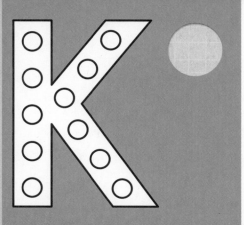

kangaroo (noun)

A **kangaroo** is an Australian animal with big back legs.

What is a baby kangaroo called?

<u>10</u>   <u>15</u>   <u>5</u>   <u>25</u>

— — —

key (noun)

A **key** is a specially-shaped piece of metal used to lock or unlock a door.

king (noun)

A **king** is a man who is born to rule a country.

Find six differences between the scenes.

knife (noun)
knives

A **knife** is a tool used for cutting. Most **knives** have a handle and a long, sharp metal blade.

koala (noun)

A **koala** is a small, furry animal from Australia. It lives in trees and eats leaves.

a b c d e f g h i j k l m n o p q r s t u v w x y z

27

A B C D E F G H I J K L M N O P Q R S T U V W X Y Z

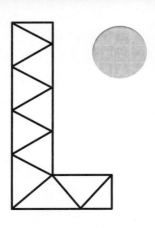

ladder (noun)

A **ladder** is something you use to climb up high. **Ladders** are made of metal or wood.

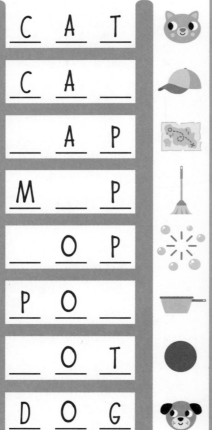

C A T
C A _
_ A P
M _ P
_ O P
P O _
_ O T
D O G

Climb the ladder by finishing the words. Fill in the blank letter on every rung, using the pictures to guide you.

28

lamp (noun)

A **lamp** is a device that gives you light. You can move a **lamp** around and switch it on and off.

Draw the other half.

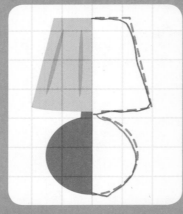

large (adjective)
larger, largest

If something is **large**, it is big. A ship is **large**. The opposite of **large** is small.

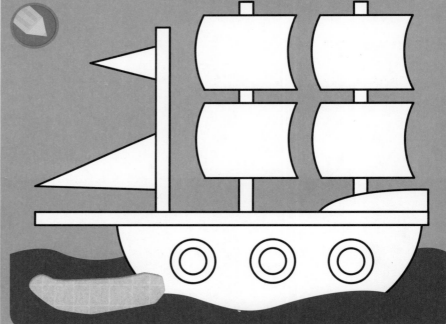

laugh (verb)
laughs, laughing, laughed

To **laugh** is to make noises because you think something is funny.

How many lamps can you see?

leaf (noun)
leaves

A **leaf** is a flat, green part of a plant, such as a tree.

Follow the line to see which tree the leaf fell from.

lemon (noun)

A **lemon** is a juicy, yellow fruit with a sour taste.

light (adjective)
lighter, lightest

1. If something is **light**, it does not weigh much. It is easy to pick up and carry. The opposite of **light** is heavy.

2. If something is **light**, it has pale colors. The opposite of **light** is dark.

lightning (noun)

Lightning is a bright, electric flash that happens during storms.

Find six differences between the scenes.

lion (noun)

A **lion** is a big, wild cat. **Lions** live in Africa and India.

What is a baby lion called?

3 21 2

___ ___ ___

listen (verb)
listens, listening, listened

To **listen** is to pay attention to a sound or to what someone is telling you.

lizard (noun)

A **lizard** is a type of animal with four legs and a long tail.

long (adjective)
longer, longest

If something is **long**, its ends are far apart. The opposite of **long** is short.

A B C D E F G H I J K L M N O P Q R S T U V W X Y Z

man (noun)
men

A **man** is a grown-up male person.

map (noun)

A **map** is a drawing that shows you where roads and other places are. You use it to find your way around.

Guide the man through the mountains.

Start →

→ Finish

mermaid (noun)

A **mermaid** is a make-believe creature that looks like a woman with a fish's tail.

Join the dots.

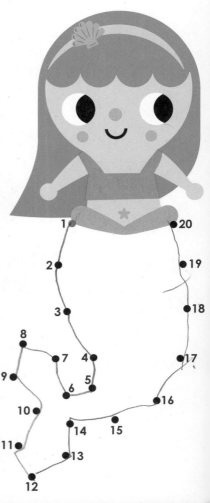

milk (noun)

Milk is a white liquid that mother animals make to feed their babies. Many people drink cows' **milk**.

money (noun)

The bills and coins that you use to buy things are types of **money**.

Which jar has the most money?

A

B

C

D

monkey (noun)

A **monkey** is a hairy animal that lives in trees. It has a long tail that helps it climb.

monster (noun)

A **monster** is a scary, make-believe creature.

Draw the other half.

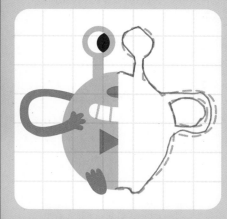

Press out and make the mini monsters from the card pages.

moon (noun)

The **moon** shines in the sky at night. It is a big ball of rock that moves slowly around Earth about once a month.

mountain (noun)

A **mountain** is a very tall, sloped piece of land. It is like a very big hill.

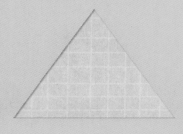

mouse (noun)
mice

A **mouse** is a small, furry animal with a long tail. **Mice** have sharp front teeth for gnawing food.

mushroom (noun)

A **mushroom** is a living thing that looks like a little umbrella. You can eat some **mushrooms**; others are poisonous.

music (noun)

Music is the sound that people make when they sing or play instruments.

What instrument is this?

2 1 14 10 15

___ ___ ___ ___ ___

A
B
C
D
E
F
G
H
I
J
K
L
M
N
O
P
Q
R
S
T
U
V
W
X
Y
Z

needle (noun)

A **needle** is a long, thin piece of metal used for sewing. It is sharp at one end and has a hole for thread at the other.

nest (noun)

A **nest** is the home that animals such as birds and mice make for their babies.

Follow the lines to see which bird lives in the nest.

net (noun)

A **net** is something made from pieces of string or rope tied together with holes in between. **Nets** are used to catch fish and for games such as tennis and basketball.

Count the balls in each net, then circle the answer below.

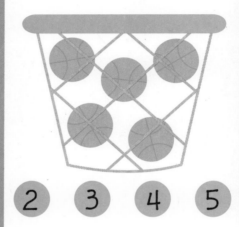

2   3   4   5

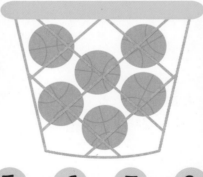

5   6   7   8

6   7   8   9

new (adjective)

newer, newest

If something is **new**, it has just been made. It is not old or worn. The opposite of **new** is old.

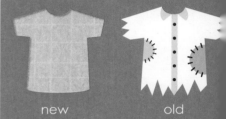

new   old

newt (noun)

A **newt** is a small animal with a long tail. It lives in water and on land.

night (noun)

Night is the time of day between evening and morning. At **night**, it is dark outside.

noise (noun)

A **noise** is a sound or sounds that are especially loud.

number (noun)

A **number** tells you how many you have of something. Both 3 and 100 are **numbers**.

Finish the number puzzles on this page.

Draw three more orange fish. How many orange fish are there now? _____

Color the picture. Use the key as a guide.

1 green	**2** pink	**3** yellow	**4** red

What is this animal?

<u>19</u> <u>5</u> <u>1</u> <u>8</u> <u>15</u> <u>18</u> <u>19</u> <u>5</u>

___ ___ ___ ___ ___ ___ ___ ___

nurse (noun)

A **nurse** is a person who takes care of people who are sick or hurt. **Nurses** often work in hospitals.

Find six differences between the scenes.

a b c d e f g h i j k l m n o p q r s t u v w x y z

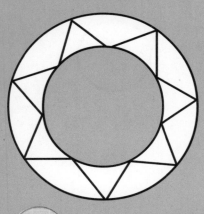

object (noun)

An **object** is a thing that takes up space and can be seen or touched.

Draw the other half of each object.

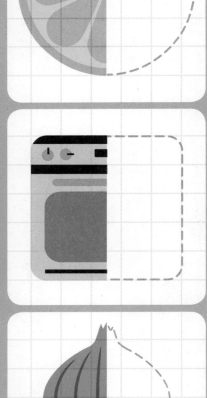

ocean (noun)

An **ocean** is a mass of saltwater that covers some of Earth's surface.

Find the ocean names in the word search. Words can go across or down.

octopus (noun)
octopuses

An **octopus** is a sea creature with eight arms.

Find six differences between the scenes.

	v	m	u	z	p		
k	a	p	a	c	i	f	i	c	a
n	q	i	s	o	u	f	n	p	r	u
a	t	l	a	n	t	i	c	d	l	c	i
t	u	v	n	u	i	n	d	i	n	t	z
i	u	g	c	r	l	b	a	u	i	e
s	o	u	t	h	e	r	n	o	c
	r	f	n	t	i

1 Atlantic   **2** Arctic   **3** Indian

4 Southern   **5** Pacific

old (noun)
older, oldest

If something is **old**, it was made or born long ago. **Old** people have been alive for a long time. The opposites of **old** are new and young.

opposite (noun)

An **opposite** is something that is completely different from something else. The **opposite** of over is under.

Draw a line to match the opposite words.

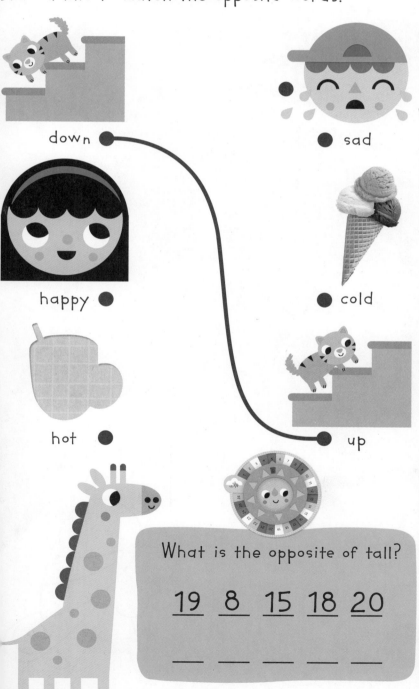

down

sad

happy

cold

hot

up

What is the opposite of tall?

<u>19</u> <u>8</u> <u>15</u> <u>18</u> <u>20</u>

___ ___ ___ ___ ___

orange (noun)

1. An **orange** is a round, juicy fruit with **orange**-colored peel.

(adjective)

2. **Orange** is a color. This carrot is **orange**.

ostrich (noun)
ostriches

An **ostrich** is a large bird with a long neck. It cannot fly.

oven (noun)

An **oven** is the part of an appliance where you roast or bake food.

owl (noun)

An **owl** is a bird that hunts for small animals at night. It has big eyes to help it see in the dark.

A B C D E F G H I J K L M N O P Q R S T U V W X Y Z

P

paint (noun)

Paint is a colored liquid that you brush onto things to change their color or to make a picture.

pair (noun)

A **pair** of things are two things that go together. We wear a **pair** of socks.

Sticker the matching pairs of socks.

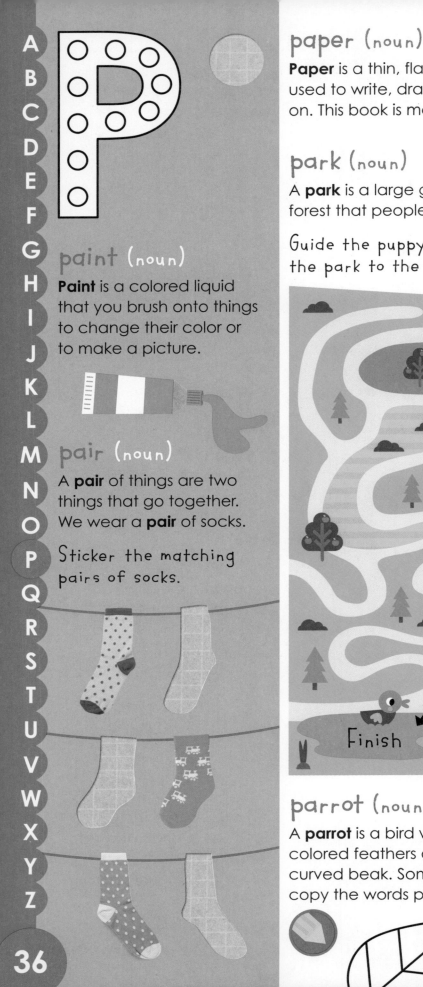

paper (noun)

Paper is a thin, flat material used to write, draw, or paint on. This book is made of **paper**.

park (noun)

A **park** is a large garden or forest that people can visit.

Guide the puppy through the park to the pond.

Start

Finish

parrot (noun)

A **parrot** is a bird with brightly colored feathers and a sharp, curved beak. Some **parrots** copy the words people speak.

party (noun)
parties

A **party** is an event where people get together to have fun. Some people have birthday **parties**.

pattern (noun)

A **pattern** is a repeating arrangement of colors, shapes, or figures.

Sticker to finish the patterns.

pencil (noun)

A **pencil** is a long, thin stick of wood with black graphite or colored wax in the middle. **Pencils** are used for writing and drawing.

Circle the two sets of coloring pencils that match.

penguin (noun)

A **penguin** is a seabird with black-and-white feathers. It lives on cold coastlines. It cannot fly but uses its wings as flippers to swim.

Draw the other half.

pet (noun)

A **pet** is a tame animal that you take care of at home. Dogs, cats, fish, and hamsters are often kept as **pets**.

a b c d e f g h i j k l m n o p q r s t u v w x y z

picture (noun)

A **picture** is a drawing, painting, or photo of something.

Search the picture for the things below. Check them as you find them.

1 barn ☐
2 dogs ☐
3 cars ☐

4 goats ☐
5 cows ☐
6 hens ☐

pig (noun)

A **pig** is an animal with a fat body, short legs, and a curly tail.

pirate (noun)

A **pirate** is a sailor who attacks and robs other sailors at sea.

plant (noun)

A **plant** is a living thing that grows in soil or in water. Trees, flowers, and grass are all **plants**.

police officer (noun)

A **police officer** is someone who keeps people safe and makes sure people obey the law.

Join the dots.

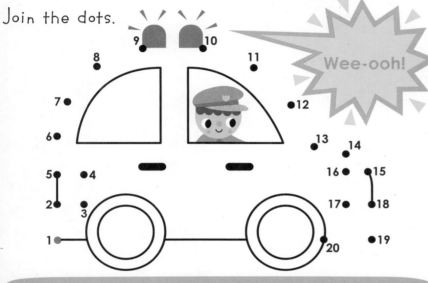

Wee-ooh!

What makes the noise on the police car?

<u>19</u>　<u>9</u>　<u>18</u>　<u>5</u>　<u>14</u>

___　___　___　___　___

present (noun)

A **present** is a gift. It is something special that you give to someone to make them happy.

Follow the lines to see which pig gets the present. Write the letter.

A

B　C

prince (noun)

A **prince** is the son of a king or queen.

princess (noun)

princesses

A **princess** is the daughter of a king or queen.

pumpkin (noun)

A **pumpkin** is a large fruit with orange skin.

Q

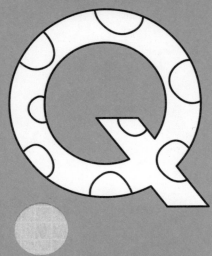

quarter (noun)

When something is broken into four pieces of the same size, one piece is called a **quarter**.

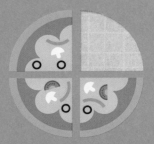

queen (noun)

A **queen** is a woman who is born to rule a country.

question (noun)

A **question** is what you ask when you want to know something.

What animal is this?

 2   1   20

___ ___ ___

quick (adjective)

quicker, quickest

To be **quick** is to move or do something fast. The opposite of **quick** is slow.

quiet (adjective)

quieter, quietest

To be **quiet** is to make very little noise. Someone or something that is **quiet** is hard to hear. The opposites of **quiet** are loud and noisy.

R

rabbit (noun)

A **rabbit** is a small, furry animal with long ears and a fluffy tail.

Follow the lines to see which rabbit reaches the carrot first.

rain (noun)

Rain is lots of little drops of water that fall from the clouds.

rhinoceros (noun)
rhinoceroses

A **rhinoceros** is a big animal with tough, leathery skin, and one or two horns on its head.

Search the grid for the word "rhinoceros."

r	h	i	n	o	c	e	r	o	s	r
e	o	r	h	o	c	i	n	r	o	c
i	r	h	i	n	o	c	e	r	o	s
r	h	i	n	o	c	e	r	o	s	x
r	h	n	e	r	i	n	s	o	u	s
i	r	h	i	n	o	c	e	r	o	s
				r	h	n	i	o
				s	e	r	r	n

How many can you see?

ring (noun)

A **ring** is a round piece of jewelry you wear on a finger.

How many rings can you see?

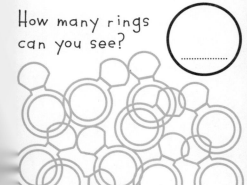

Circle two rings that match.

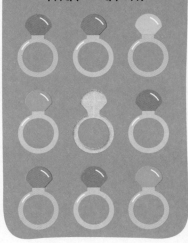

road (noun)

A **road** is a long, hard piece of land that people travel along to reach other places.

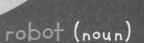

robot (noun)

A **robot** is a machine that can do some of the jobs that people do.

rocket (noun)

A **rocket** is the part of a spacecraft that pushes it high into space.

a b c d e f g h i j k l m n o p q r s t u v w x y z

41

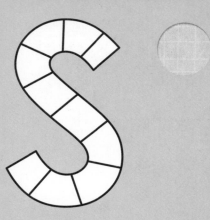

sad (adjective)

sadder, saddest

To feel **sad** is to be upset or down. The opposite of **sad** is happy.

sandwich (noun)

sandwiches

A **sandwich** is something you eat that is made of two slices of bread with a filling, such as cheese or ham.

Draw the other half.

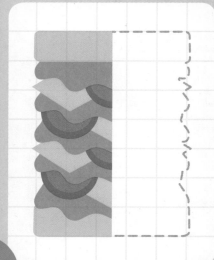

scarf (noun)

scarves

A **scarf** is something you wear around your neck to keep warm.

school (noun)

A **school** is a place where children go to learn about things like reading, writing, and counting.

season (noun)

A **season** is one of the four natural parts of the year. The four **seasons** are spring, summer, fall, and winter.

spring

summer

fall

winter

shadow (noun)

A **shadow** is a shaded shape on the ground or surfaces caused by something blocking out the light.

Find the shadow that matches this shape.

shark (noun)

A **shark** is a type of big fish. **Sharks** hunt other sea creatures for food.

sheep (noun)

sheep

A **sheep** is an animal with a thick, woolly coat. Male **sheep** are called rams, females are called ewes, and babies are called lambs.

Draw legs and heads to finish these sheep.

shell (noun)

A **shell** is a thin, hard covering around something. Shellfish, snails, eggs, and nuts have shells.

How many shells can you see? ....

shoe (noun)

Shoes are things you wear on your feet to keep them safe and dry.

short (noun)

shorter, shortest

If something is **short**, its top is close to its bottom. The opposites of **short** are tall and long.

skate (verb)

skates, skating, skated

To **skate** is to glide over smooth ground wearing **skates**, which have blades or wheels on the bottom.

Follow the lines to discover which skater won the trophy. Write the letter.

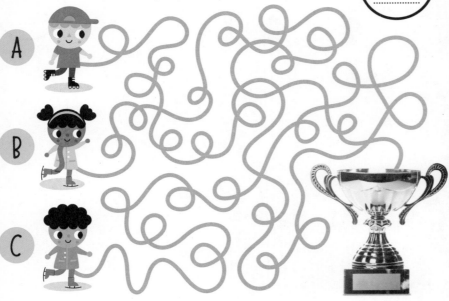

skeleton (noun)

A **skeleton** is all the bones that make up a person or animal's body.

Sticker to make the skeletons match.

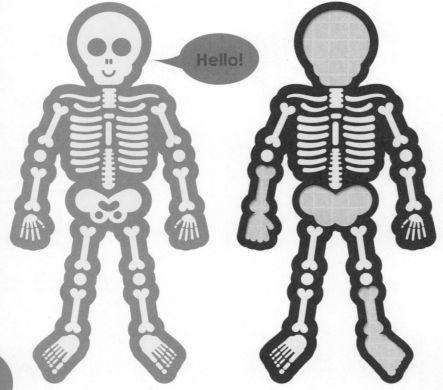

Hello!

skirt (noun)

A **skirt** is a piece of clothing that hangs from your waist and covers all or part of your legs.

Circle the one that doesn't belong.

sleep (verb)

sleeps, sleeping, slept

When you **sleep**, you close your eyes and rest deeply. You often dream when you **sleep**.

Draw what the puppy is dreaming of.

slide (noun)

A **slide** is a smooth surface that people move down.

A B C D E F G H I J K L M N O P Q R S T U V W X Y Z

slow (adjective)

slower, slowest

If something is **slow**, it takes a long time to do something. A **slow** car takes a long time to get places. The opposites of **slow** are fast and quick.

small (adjective)

smaller, smallest

If something is **small**, it is little. The opposites of **small** are big and large.

snail (noun)

A **snail** is a small animal with a shell on its back. It has no legs and moves by sliding on a large foot.

Find six differences between the scenes.

snake (noun)

A **snake** has a long body and no legs. Its skin is scaly.

A snake smells with its ...

<u>20</u> <u>15</u> <u>14</u> <u>7</u> <u>21</u> <u>5</u>

___ ___ ___ ___ ___

snow (noun)

Snow is made of fluffy, white ice crystals that fall from the sky.

snowman (noun)

snowmen

A **snowman** is made of snow and shaped like a person.

Circle the snowmen to answer the questions.

1 Who has lost their nose?

2 Whose scarf is yellow?

3 Who is asleep?

a b c d e f g h i j k l m n o p q r s t u v w x y z

45

sock (noun)

Socks are things you wear on your feet to keep them warm.

Circle the two socks that match.

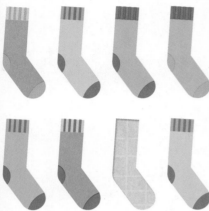

space (noun)

Space is the rest of the universe beyond Earth. There is no air in **space**.

Find six differences between the scenes.

spider (noun)

A **spider** is a small animal with eight legs. Most **spiders** spin webs to catch insects for food.

Guide the spider through the maze to the fly.

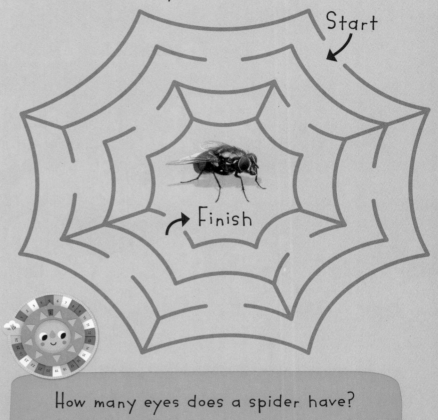

Start

Finish

How many eyes does a spider have?

<u>5</u> <u>9</u> <u>7</u> <u>8</u> <u>20</u>

__ __ __ __ __

spoon (noun)

A **spoon** is a tool used for eating. It has a long handle and a round end. You use a **spoon** to eat foods such as soup and cereal.

How many spoons can you see?

46

squirrel (noun)

A **squirrel** is a small, furry animal that lives in trees. It has a bushy tail and eats nuts.

Copy the squirrel. Use the grid to guide you.

steal (verb)

steals, stealing, stole, stolen

To **steal** is to take something that does not belong to you without asking.

Join the dots to see who stole the bananas.

strawberry (noun)

strawberries

A **strawberry** is a soft, sweet ed fruit with seeds on it.

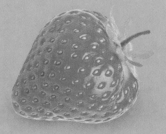

sun (noun)

The **sun** is a close star that shines in the sky and gives Earth light and heat. Earth moves around the **sun**.

supermarket (noun)

A **supermarket** is a large store that sells many different kinds of food.

swan (noun)

A **swan** is a large bird with a long neck. It lives on rivers and lakes.

Use stickers to finish the picture.

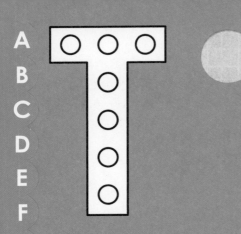

table (noun)

A **table** is a piece of furniture with legs and a flat top. You can eat or work at a **table**.

Find six differences between the scenes.

tadpole (noun)

A **tadpole** is a young frog or toad. It hatches with gills and a tail but no legs.

tail (noun)

An animal's **tail** grows at the end of its body. It helps the animal balance.

talk (verb)

talks, talking, talked

To **talk** is to speak, or to use words, out loud.

What is the bear saying?

<u>9</u> <u>1</u> <u>13</u> <u>8</u> <u>21</u> <u>14</u> <u>7</u> <u>18</u> <u>25</u>

_____

tall (adjective)

taller, tallest

If something is **tall**, its top is high above the ground. The opposite of **tall** is short.

taste (verb)

tastes, tasting, tasted

To **taste** something is to find out what it is like by putting it in your mouth.

teacher (noun)

A **teacher** is a person who helps other people learn things.

Search the page for the words and fill in the missing letters.

```
T _ I L
T A _ K
T E N _
```

telephone (noun)

A **telephone** is a machine you use to talk to someone in another place.

How many telephones can you see? ....

television (noun)

A **television** is a machine that shows pictures on a screen and also has sounds.

Draw your favorite television program on the screen.

tent (noun)

A **tent** is a shelter made of a piece of cloth stretched over poles. You use a **tent** for camping.

There are three people in each tent. How many people are camping in total? Write the answer. ....

thunder (noun)

Thunder is a loud sound in the air that you hear after lightning.

tiger (noun)

A **tiger** is a big, wild cat with orange-and-black striped fur. Wild **tigers** are rare, but some still live in India and China.

Draw stripes on the tiger.

See p. 64 to learn how to make the press-out tiger model.

Terrific tiger

tiny (adjective)

tinier, tiniest

If something is **tiny**, it is very small. The opposite of **tiny** is huge.

tired (adjective)

more tired, most tired
To be **tired** is to need a rest or to feel sleepy.

tomato (noun)

tomatoes

A **tomato** is a soft, round red fruit that people often eat in salads.

Count the tomatoes in each basket.
Circle the answer.

7   8   9

8   9   10

tool (noun)

A **tool** is something you use to make work easier. Wrenches, screwdrivers, and hammers are all **tools**.

Find the words in the word search. Words can go across or down.

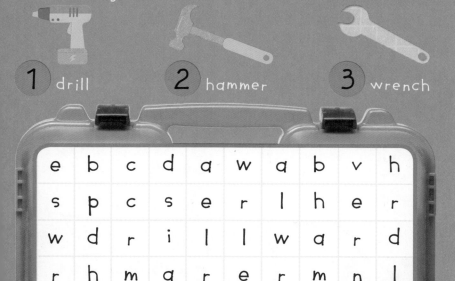

1 drill 2 hammer 3 wrench

e	b	c	d	a	w	a	b	v	h
s	p	c	s	e	r	l	h	e	r
w	d	r	i	l	l	w	a	r	d
r	h	m	a	r	e	r	m	n	l
n	e	c	h	w	r	h	m	o	l
w	r	e	n	c	h	a	e	t	i
c	n	r	c	w	r	e	r	m	m

toothbrush (noun)

toothbrushes

You use a **toothbrush** with toothpaste to keep your teeth clean.

Circle two toothbrushes that match.

toy (noun)

A **toy** is something you play with. Dolls, building blocks, teddy bears, and train sets are all **toys**.

What is this toy?

<u>11</u> <u>9</u> <u>20</u> <u>5</u>

___ ___ ___ ___

tractor (noun)

A **tractor** is a farm vehicle with big black wheels. It is often used to pull things.

Follow the lines to see which tractor drives to the tree.

tree (noun)

A **tree** is a tall plant with leaves, branches, and a thick wooden stem, called a trunk.

truck (noun)

A **truck** is a large, strong vehicle that takes things from one place to another.

a b c d e f g h i j k l m n o p q r s t u v w x y z

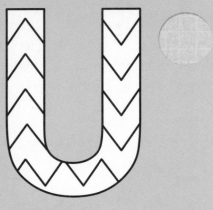

umbrella (noun)

You hold an **umbrella** over your head to keep yourself dry when it rains.

underwear (noun)

We call the clothes that we wear under all our other clothes **underwear**. Briefs are **underwear**.

unicorn (noun)

A **unicorn** is a make-believe animal that looks like a horse with a horn on its head.

vacuum cleaner (noun)

A **vacuum cleaner** is a machine that sucks up dust and dirt.

vase (noun)

A **vase** is a container that you can use to hold cut flowers in water.

vegetable (noun)

A **vegetable** is part of a plant that can be eaten. We cook **vegetables** and also eat some raw. Cabbages, carrots, and onions are **vegetables**.

violin (noun)

A **violin** is a musical instrument made of wood. You play it using a bow.

volcano (noun)
volcanoes

A **volcano** is a mountain that sometimes erupts, sending out gases and melted, or molten, rocks.

Draw the other half.

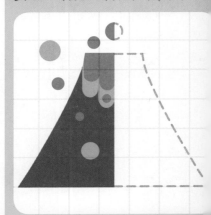

walk (verb)
walks, walking, walked

To **walk** is to move along by putting one foot forward and then the other.

Find six differences between the scenes.

wash (noun)
washes, washing, washed

To **wash** something is to make it clean. We **wash** our hands with soap and water. We **wash** clothes in a washing machine.

watch (noun)
watches

A **watch** is a small clock that you can wear on your wrist. It tells you what time it is.

Follow the lines to discover who owns the watch.

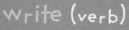

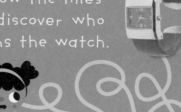

wolf (noun)
wolves

A **wolf** is a wild animal that looks a little like a large dog.

woman (noun)
women

A **woman** is a grown-up female person.

write (verb)
writes, writing, wrote, written

To **write** is to use a pencil or a pen to record words or numbers.

What has been written on the notepad?

<u>23</u> <u>1</u> <u>19</u> <u>8</u>

___ ___ ___

<u>19</u> <u>15</u> <u>3</u> <u>11</u> <u>19</u>

___

X

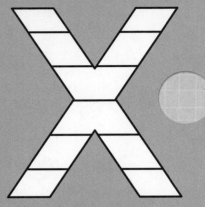

x-ray (noun)

An **x-ray** is a picture that lets a doctor or dentist see inside your body.

xylophone (noun)

A **xylophone** is a musical instrument with a row of bars of different lengths.

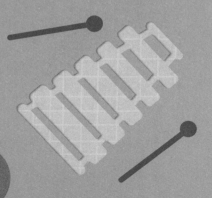

Y

yacht (noun)

A **yacht** is a boat with sails or an engine.

yawn (verb)

yawns, yawning, yawned
When you **yawn**, you open your mouth wide and breathe in.

yogurt (noun)

Yogurt is a food made from milk. It is often mixed with fruit.

Circle two yogurt pots that match.

yolk (noun)

The **yolk** is the middle part of an egg. It is orange.

young (adjective)
younger, youngest

To be **young** is to have lived for only a short time. Children are **young**. The opposite of **young** is old.

yo-yo (noun)

A **yo-yo** is a round toy that you roll up and down on a string.

Follow the lines to see who has the blue yo-yo.

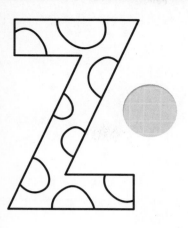

zebra (noun)

A **zebra** is an animal that looks like a horse with black-and-white stripes. **Zebras** live in Africa.

Find six differences between the scenes.

zipper (noun)

A **zipper** joins two pieces of material together. The **zipper's** teeth lock together when you close it.

zoo (noun)

A **zoo** is a place where people can go to see wild animals.

What animal is hiding in the bush?

2 5 1 18

___ ___ ___ ___

a b c d e f g h i j k l m n o p q r s t u v w x y z

Colors and shapes

Answer the questions and solve the
puzzles to practice your colors and shapes.

Color the picture.
Use the key as a guide.

1 pink
2 red
3 orange
4 yellow
5 green
6 blue

Draw the other half, then color it.

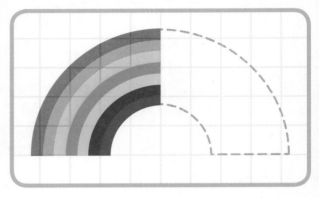

Circle two paint pots that match.

How many purple
hats can you see?

Search the grid for the shape words.
Words can go across or down.

t	r	n	i	g	l	a	y	u	x	t	o	v	l
d	m	i	a	s	q	r	a	s	l	o	a	h	r
r	c	e	n	q	c	i	k	t	h	v	b	e	a
s	w	q	h	u	y	r	e	a	z	a	y	t	s
u	a	n	e	a	s	c	i	r	c	l	e	n	s
e	r	g	a	r	m	r	r	t	r	a	c	m	w
s	d	p	r	e	c	t	a	n	g	l	e	p	a
v	a	l	t	r	i	a	n	g	l	e	h	q	r
h	e	a	s	m	r	v	w	h	m	q	u	u	p
i	a	m	n	d	i	a	m	o	n	d	j	s	d
s	i	z	t	r	a	r	n	m	e	c	o	v	l

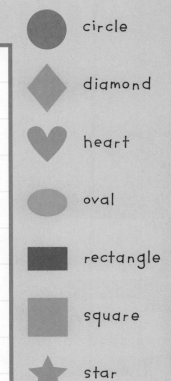

- circle
- diamond
- heart
- oval
- rectangle
- square
- star
- triangle

Sticker shapes to create a cool monster.

Guide the monster through the shape maze.

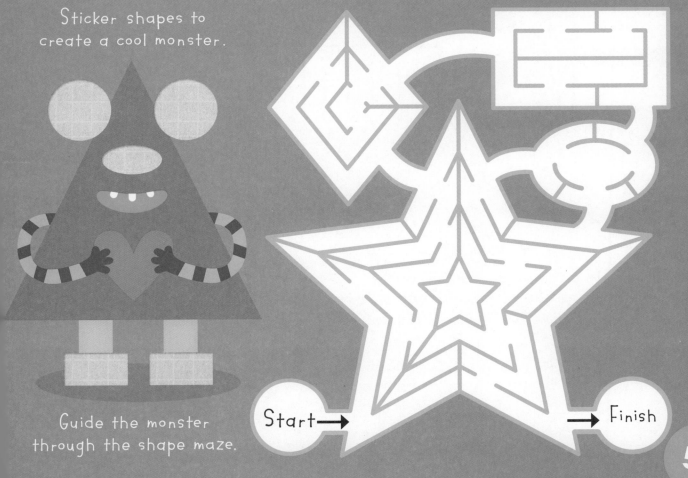

Start → → Finish

Animals and numbers

Answer the questions and solve the puzzles to practice your animal names and numbers.

Fill in the blank letters to complete the crossword. Each word is an animal name. Search for the animal names in the dictionary, using the clues to guide you.

Circle six spiders hiding on the page.

2 Find me on page 19.

3 Find me on page 53.

4 Find me on page 23.

5 Find me on page 43.

6 Find me on page 50.

1 J
2 _ _ E _ H _ _ _ T **6**
3 _ O L _
4 _ I R _ F _ E
5 S _ _ _ _ K
J E L L Y F I S H
T G _ _

Draw the other half.

What is a baby sheep called?

12 1 13 2

___ ___ ___ ___

What is a baby horse called?

6 15 1 12

___ ___ ___ ___

Answer the animal questions. Draw a line from the animal to the correct number on the number line.

How many ears do I have?

How many bananas do I have?

How many spots do I have?

How many arms do I have?

How many insects are there?

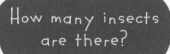

1	one
2	two
3	three
4	four
5	five
6	six
7	seven
8	eight
9	nine
10	ten
11	eleven
12	twelve
13	thirteen
14	fourteen
15	fifteen
16	sixteen
17	seventeen
18	eighteen
19	nineteen
20	twenty

How many stripes do I have?

Days and months

Answer the questions and solve the puzzles to practice knowing the days of the week and months in the year.

There are seven days in a week. You can use a calendar to track the days in a month. Find six differences between the calendars.

MONDAY	**MONDAY**
TUESDAY	**TUESDAY**
WEDNESDAY	**SATURDAY**
THURSDAY	**THURSDAY**
FRIDAY	**FRIDAY**
SATURDAY	**SATURDAY**
SUNDAY	**SUNDAY**

There are twelve months in a year. The months are split into four seasons. Finish the activities for each season.

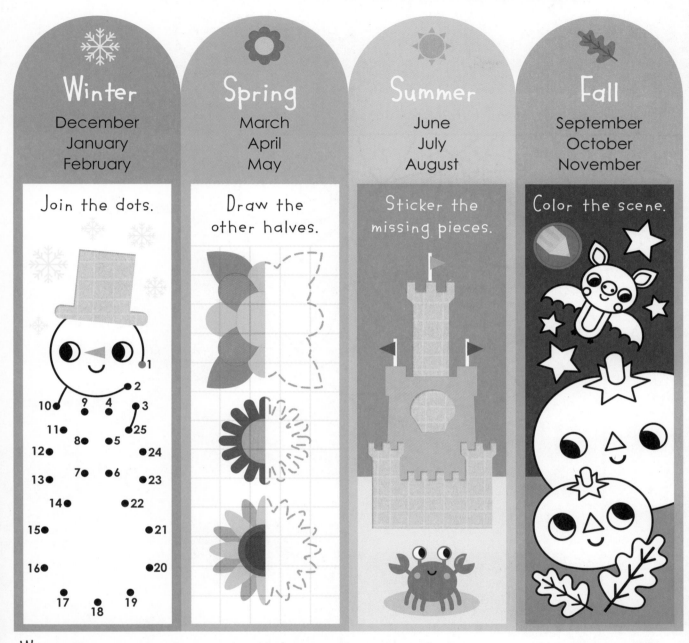

Winter
December
January
February

Join the dots.

Spring
March
April
May

Draw the other halves.

Summer
June
July
August

Sticker the missing pieces.

Fall
September
October
November

Color the scene.

Write the month of your birthday in the space below.

. . . .

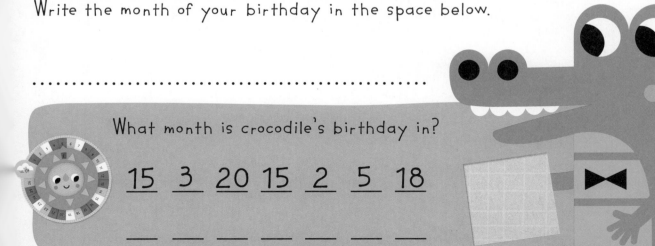

What month is crocodile's birthday in?

<u>15</u> <u>3</u> <u>20</u> <u>15</u> <u>2</u> <u>5</u> <u>18</u>

___ ___ ___ ___ ___ ___ ___

Fruit and vegetables

Answer the questions and solve the puzzles
to learn about fruit and vegetables.

Color the fruit bowl, using the dots as a guide.

What fruits can you see?

....

....

Draw the other half.

What is your
favorite fruit?

....

Search the shopping bag for the fruit
below. Circle them when you find them.

5 cherries

3 bananas

2 lemons

4 pears

4 apples

6 strawberries

Search the grid for the vegetable words below. Words can go across or down.

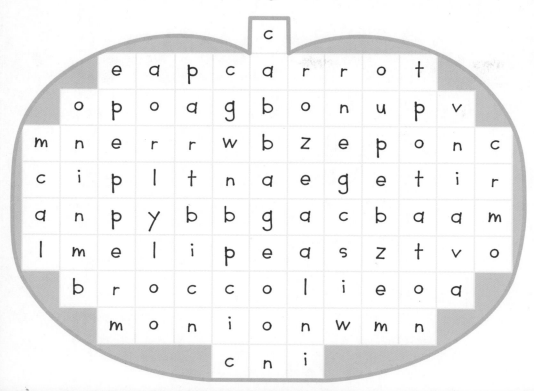

				c						
e	a	p	c	a	r	r	o	t		
o	p	o	a	g	b	o	n	u	p	v
m	n	e	r	r	w	b	z	e	p	o	n	c
c	i	p	l	t	n	a	e	g	e	t	i	r
a	n	p	y	b	b	g	a	c	b	a	a	m
l	m	e	l	i	p	e	a	s	z	t	v	o
b	r	o	c	c	o	l	i	e	o	a
m	o	n	i	o	n	w	m	n
	c	n	i			

 broccoli

 cabbage

 carrot

 onion

 peas

 pepper

potato

Hello!

Hi!

What is sweet corn also known as?

 13 1 9 26 5

___ ___ ___ ___ ___

Find six differences between the scenes.

63

How to use your card pages

Code wheel

1. Press out the big wheel, the small wheel, the window, and the center.

2. Place the small wheel on top of the big wheel. Align the window so you can see the sun's face, and then turn the small wheel to reveal the letters in the window.

Cartoon stencils

Press out the cartoon stencils. Draw around them and doodle details to create your own cool cartoons!

Perfect pairs

1. Press out the cards and place them facedown on the table.

2. Turn over two cards at a time. If they match, put them to one side. If they don't, turn them over and try again.

3. Keep going until you've found all the pairs!

Mini monsters

1. To make one monster, press out a monster shape and open the slits. Then press out the arms.

2. Fold and curl the monster shape into a box, then slot the backs together as shown.

3. Slide the arms through the slits to finish.

Terrific tiger

1. Press out the tiger shapes.

2. Ask an adult to help you hold the side pieces in place, and then position the face pieces above the slits.

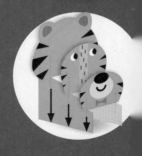

3. Slot face shape A into the slit at the back of the side pieces. Slot face shape B into the slit in the middle of the side pieces. Slot face shape C into the slit at the front of the side pieces.

Stickers for pages 4-5

What's that noise?

pages 6-7

pages 10-11

pages 8-9

pages 12-13

pages 14–15

purple

orange

pages 16–17

d

pages 18–19

e

pages 20–21

f

pages 22–23

g

pages 24–25

h

page 26

i j

FIRE

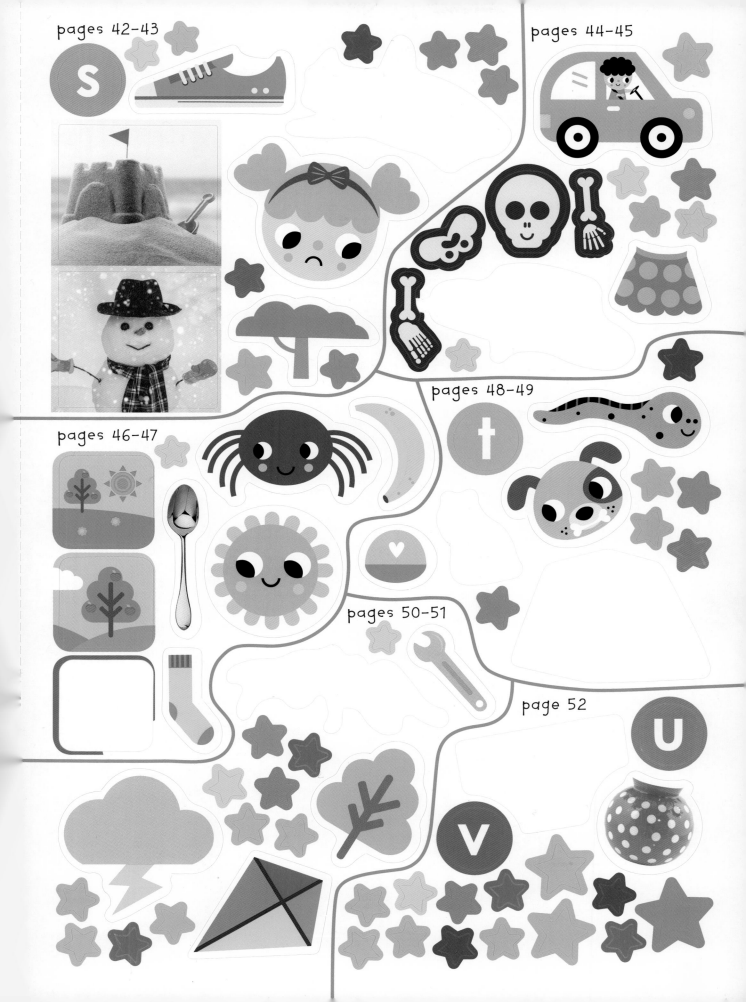

pages 42–43

pages 44–45

pages 48–49

pages 46–47

pages 50–51

page 52

page 53

pages 54–55

pages 56–57

pages 58–59

pages 62–63

pages 60–61

Extra stickers

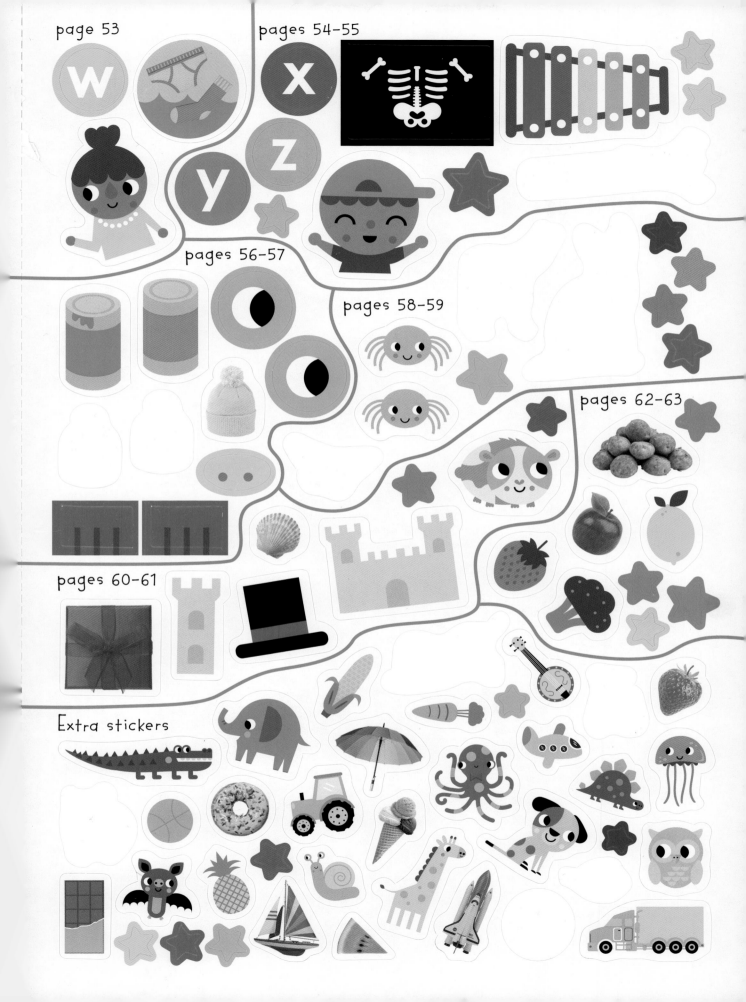

Extra stickers